STUDENT GUIDE

CHANCE ENCOUNTERS

PROBABILITY IN GAMES AND SIMULATIONS

MathScape™
SEEING AND THINKING
MATHEMATICALLY

P.41 4,5,6,7

ALLPLAY

PHASE**ONE**

Games of Chance and Probability

In this phase, you will explore the meaning of chance. You will play different booths at a carnival using coins and cubes, and investigate one of the booths in depth. Using strip graphs, frequency graphs, and probability lines, you will learn to show chance visually.

What mathematics is involved in testing and analyzing games of chance?

CHANCE ENCOUNTERS

PHASE**TWO**
Spinner Games and Probability

Games played with circular spinners are the focus of this phase. You will experiment with ways of changing games to improve your chances of scoring. To solve the Mystery Spinner Game, you will create spinners to match a set of clues. The clues describe probabilities in words and numbers. Finally you will be ready to design your own Mystery Spinner Game.

PHASE**THREE**
Fair and Unfair Games

How can you tell if a game is fair? To test your predictions about how fair a game is, you will conduct experiments. You will learn to use outcome grids to determine the probability of outcomes in a game. Your understanding of fractions, decimals, and percentages will help you to compare the probabilities of scoring in games.

PHASE**FOUR**
Real-World Simulations

Your final project is to design, test, and present your own simulation game. But first, you will test and design other simulation games. In a Miniature Golf Simulation, you will compare your results to actual data from that game. In the Shape Toss Game, you will collect data by tossing a penny. Then you will create a simulation to match your game results.

PHASE ONE

To: Apprentice Game Designers
From: AllPlay Company Directors

Your first assignment is to work on six new booths in the Carnival Collection. We have designed a rough draft, and now it is time to test it.

It's hard to tell about a booth from just one person's experience. That's why we want all of you to try the booths and tell us what you think. We want your ideas on how to improve them.

AllPlay

In this phase, you will test games of chance. By learning about probability, you will be able to analyze the chances of winning.

To help you in your role as game tester and designer, you can think about how likely it is that certain events will happen every day. Do you think what happens to you is due to chance or luck?

Games of Chance and Probability

WHAT'S THE MATH?

Investigations in this section focus on:

THEORETICAL and EXPERIMENTAL PROBABILITY

- Understanding the concept of chance

- Conducting probability experiments

- Determining the theoretical probability and experimental probability of events

MULTIPLE REPRESENTATIONS of PROBABILITY

- Representing data with frequency and strip graphs

- Describing probabilities with qualitative terms, such as *likely, unlikely,* and *always*

- Describing probabilities quantitatively with decimals, fractions, and percentages

MODELING SITUATIONS with SIMULATIONS

- Ranking event probabilities on a scale of 0 to 1

1 The Carnival Collection

EXPLORING GAMES OF CHANCE

The AllPlay Company is developing games of chance designed as booths in the Carnival Collection. You will test the Carnival Collection and graph the class results. Can you come up with ideas for improving the Carnival Collection?

Test the Carnival Collection

What can you find out about games by comparing the experiences of many players?

Play the Carnival Collection with a partner. Each player should make a score sheet. For each turn, record the name of the booth and whether or not you scored a point.

The Carnival Collection

Players take turns. On your turn, pick the booth you want to play. You can choose a different booth or stay at the same booth on each turn. The player with the most points at the end of ten turns wins.

- Get Ahead Booth: Toss a coin. Heads scores 1 point.

- Lucky 3s Booth: Roll a number cube. A roll of 3 scores 1 point.

- Evens or Odds Booth: Roll a number cube. A roll of 2, 4, or 6 scores 1 point.

- Pick a Number Booth: Predict what number you will roll. Then roll a number cube. A true prediction scores 1 point.

- Coin and Cube Booth: Toss a coin and roll a number cube. Tails and 3, 4, 5, or 6 scores 1 point.

- Teens Only Booth: Roll a number cube 2 times. Make a 2-digit number with the digits in any order. A roll of 13, 14, 15, or 16 scores 1 point.

Design a Winning Strategy

Use the graph of your class results to help you design a strategy that would give players a good chance of scoring points in the Carnival Collection.

1 Which booths would you go to? Why?

2 How many points do you think a player would be likely to score in 10 turns by using your strategy? Explain your thinking.

3 How many points do you think a player would be likely to score in 100 turns by using your strategy? Show how you know.

Which booths give you the best chances of scoring points?

Improve the Carnival Collection

Use what you have learned to improve the Carnival Collection.

1 Pick one booth at which you think it is too hard to score points. Change the booth to make it *more likely* for players to score points.

2 Pick one booth at which you think it is too easy to score points. Change the booth to make it *less likely* for players to score points.

3 Design a new booth that uses coins and/or number cubes. What do you think the chances are of scoring points at the booth? Explain your thinking.

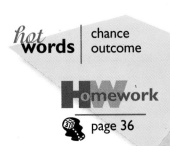

hot **words** | chance
outcome

Homework

page 36

2 Coins and Cubes Experiment

Would everyone get the same results in 20 turns at the same booth in the Carnival Collection? To find out, your class will choose one booth and conduct an experiment on it. You will make predictions, gather data, and graph the data.

What can an experiment tell you about your chances of scoring in a game?

Conduct an Experiment

Write down your predictions about the booth your class has chosen to test. How many points do you think you will get in 20 turns at the booth? What do you think the greatest number of points in the class will be? the least? What do you think the most common number of points will be? After making your predictions, conduct an experiment.

1 With a partner, take turns playing the booth. Before each toss of a coin or cube, predict what you will get.

2 After each turn, record the results on a strip graph as shown. Color the box for that turn if you scored a point. Leave the box blank if you did not score. Play for 20 turns.

H	T	H	H	H	T	T	H	T	T	H	H	H	H	H	T	H	H	T	T	T

3 Record the total number of points and greatest number of points scored in a row.

Summarize the Results

Use the results from your class's strip graphs and frequency graph to figure out the class totals for points, no points, and tosses. Then answer the following questions:

How can you summarize the class's results?

1 Use the whole class's results to find the experimental probability for getting a point. Then find the experimental probability for your individual results. How do your results compare with the class results?

2 What is the theoretical probability of getting a point at these booths: Get Ahead, Lucky 3s, Evens or Odds, and Pick a Number? Explain how you figured it out.

3 What do the results of the class experiment tell you about the chances of winning points at the booth?

What Is Probability?

Probability describes the chances of an event occurring. For example, the *theoretical probability* of getting heads when you toss a coin is:

$$\frac{\text{Number of favorable outcomes} \longrightarrow \text{heads}}{\text{Total number of possible outcomes} \longrightarrow \text{heads and tails}} \longrightarrow \frac{1}{2}$$

It could also be written as **1** out of **2**, **50%**, or **0.5**.

To figure out *experimental probability,* you need to collect data by doing an experiment. One class tossed a coin **400** times with these results:

Number of heads: 188	Number of tails: 212	Number of tosses: 400

Based on that class's results, the experimental probability of getting heads is:

$$\frac{\begin{array}{c}\text{Total number of times the}\\ \text{favorable outcome happened}\end{array} \longrightarrow \text{heads was tossed}}{\begin{array}{c}\text{Total number of times you}\\ \text{did the experiment}\end{array} \longrightarrow \text{coin tosses}} \longrightarrow \frac{188}{400}$$

It could also be written as **188** out of **400**, **47%**, or **0.47**.

hot **words** | strip graph
frequency graph

 **H**omework

 page 37

3 From Never to Always

DESCRIBING THE LIKELIHOOD OF EVENTS

How likely are different events on a typical school day? In this lesson, you will use words and numbers to describe and compare probabilities for events. Then you will analyze the results of experiments for a new Carnival Collection booth.

Use Numbers to Represent Probabilities

How can you use percentages, fractions, and decimals to describe probabilities?

Imagine that the name of each student in your class is in a hat. The teacher will pick one name from the hat without looking.

1 Use a percentage, fraction, or decimal to describe the probability of each event:

   a. The winner is a girl.

   b. The winner is a boy.

   c. You are the winner.

   d. The winner is a student in your class.

2 Make a probability line and place the events on it.

Probability Lines

- Probability lines are useful tools for ordering events from *least likely* to *most likely* to happen.

- Events that are *impossible* and will *never* happen have a probability of 0, or 0%.

- Events that are *definite* and will *always* happen have a probability of 1, or 100%.

- A probability can never be greater than 1, or 100%.

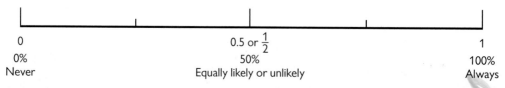

0	0.5 or $\frac{1}{2}$	1
0%	50%	100%
Never	Equally likely or unlikely	Always

Analyze a New Carnival Collection Booth

The handout High/Low Booth describes a new booth two students have designed and tested for the Carnival Collection. Use the information on the handout to write a report on the booth.

How could you use what you have learned about probability to analyze a new booth?

1 Write a summary of the class experiment that answers the following questions:

    a. What was the most common number of wins? the range of wins?

    b. How do Dan and SooKim's results compare with those of their classmates?

    c. What is the experimental probability of scoring a point, based on Dan and SooKim's data? Explain how you figured it out.

    d. What is the experimental probability of scoring a point, based on the whole class's data?

2 Figure out the theoretical probability of scoring a point.

    a. Explain how you figured out the theoretical probability.

    b. Why is the theoretical probability different from the experimental probability that you figured out?

3 Make a probability line to show the theoretical probabilities of winning a point at these three booths: High/Low, Evens or Odds, and Lucky 3s. See page 6 for the rules for Evens or Odds and Lucky 3s. Label each probability with the booth name and with a fraction, decimal, or percentage.

theoretical probability
experimental probability

omework

page 38

PHASE TWO

You might imagine yourself as a detective in this phase as you create spinners by solving sets of clues. This prepares you to design your own Mystery Spinner Game at the end of the phase. Exchanging the game you create with your classmates and playing games adds to the fun.

As you look at spinners, you will see that they show events of unequal probability. What are some ways to change a game to make the probability more equal?

Spinner Games and Probability

WHAT'S THE MATH?

Investigations in this section focus on:

THEORETICAL and EXPERIMENTAL PROBABILITY

- Conducting probability experiments
- Determining the theoretical probability of events
- Distinguishing events that have equal probabilities from events that have unequal probabilities

MULTIPLE REPRESENTATIONS of PROBABILITY

- Exploring area models of probability
- Describing probabilities with qualitative terms, such as *likely, unlikely,* and *always*
- Describing probabilities quantitatively with decimals, fractions, and percentages
- Relating verbal, visual, and numerical representations of probability

4 Spin with the Cover-Up Game

What is it like to play a game with circular spinners that have unequal parts? You will find out when you compare your results in the Cover-Up Game with those of your classmates. How can you improve the Cover-Up Game?

Design a New Game Card

How can you improve the chances of finishing the game in fewer spins?

Think about the class results from the Cover-Up Game. Use the results to help you design a new game card that will give you a good chance of finishing in the fewest spins.

- Draw a game card with 12 empty boxes.

- In each box write *red*, *blue*, or *yellow*. You do not need to use every color.

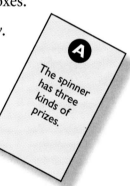

The spinner has three kinds of prizes.

The Cover-Up Game

1. Play with a partner using a spinner like the one shown. You will also need to make a Game Card and an Extras Table like the ones shown.

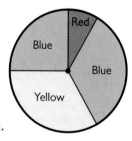

2. Take turns spinning a color. Put an X in the box of that color on your Game Card. If you do not need that color, mark a tally in the Extras Table.

3. The game ends when there's an X in every box on your Game Card. Record the number of spins you took. The goal is to make an X in all the boxes in the fewest number of spins.

Game Card

B	B	B	B
R	R	R	R
Y	Y	Y	Y

Extras Table

B	R	Y

Analyze Spinners

For each spinner shown, what are the chances of getting each part of the spinner? Use words and numbers to describe the chances.

How can you use what you know about spinners to design a new game?

Foods

Sports

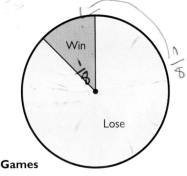

Games

How would you describe a spinner using words and numbers?

Design a New Cover-Up Game

Design your own version of the Cover-Up Game and write about what happened when you played it.

1 Design a circular spinner with 3–6 parts.

   a. Label the parts with the names of music groups, places, or whatever you'd like.

   b. Show the size of each spinner part by labeling it with a fraction.

2 Make a game card for your spinner that gives you a good chance of making an X in all of the boxes in the fewest spins.

3 Play your game and record the extras you get in a table. Record the number of spins.

4 How did you design your game? Write about why you filled in the game card the way you did.

Tip: To make a spinner, trace the circle and center point from the Cover-Up Game spinner. Then divide up the parts the way you want.

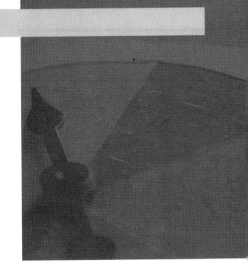

hot **words** | spinner
chance

Homework

page 39

5 The Mystery Spinner Game

DESCRIBING SPINNERS IN WORDS AND NUMBERS

How could you create a spinner using a set of clues?

This is what you will do as you play the Mystery Spinner Game. Writing about your strategies and solving problems with clue sets will help you design your own Mystery Spinner Game later on.

How can you design a spinner to match probabilities described in words and numbers?

Play the Mystery Spinner Game

After you have solved Clue Set A with the class, you will be given Mystery Spinner Game Clue Sets. Solve the Mystery Spinner Game Clue Sets in your group. Be ready to explain the strategies you used to figure out clues and design spinners.

A You have the same chances of getting a stuffed animal as getting a T-shirt.

A You are likely to win an apple about 50% of the time.

A The spinner has three kinds of prizes.

A You will probably get a T-shirt about $\frac{1}{4}$ of the time.

The Mystery Spinner Game

1. Each player gets one clue. Players read the clues aloud to the group. They cannot show their clues to one another.

2. The group draws one spinner that matches all the players' clues.

3. The group labels the parts of the spinner with fractions, decimals, or percentages.

4. The group checks to make sure the spinner matches all the clues.

Interpret Clues and Describe Strategies

Draw a circular spinner that matches Clue Set B. Label the parts with fractions, percentages, or decimals. Then answer these questions:

- What strategies did you use to make one spinner that matched all the clues?

- What kinds of clues make good starting points?

- How can you prove that your spinner matches all of the clues?

B This spinner has four kinds of sports equipment that you can win. The chances of getting a basketball are 1:6.

B You will probably get skates about 40 times in 240 spins.

B The chances of getting a Frisbee™ are about 0.33.

B You are twice as likely to get sneakers as a basketball.

Fix Sets of Clues

Explain what's wrong with Clue Sets C and D. Change the clues to fix the problems. Then draw a spinner to match each set of corrected clues.

How can you fix clues that are misleading?

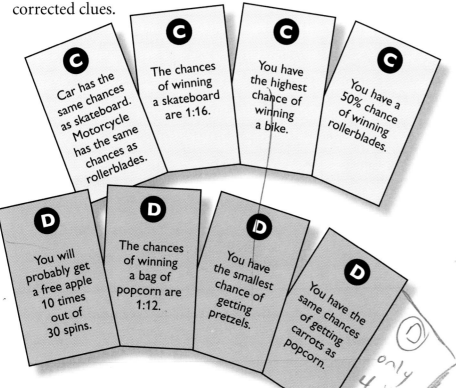

C Car has the same chances as skateboard. Motorcycle has the same chances as rollerblades.

C The chances of winning a skateboard are 1:16.

C You have the highest chance of winning a bike.

C You have a 50% chance of winning rollerblades.

D You will probably get a free apple 10 times out of 30 spins.

D The chances of winning a bag of popcorn are 1:12.

D You have the smallest chance of getting pretzels.

D You have the same chances of getting carrots as popcorn.

 *hot* **words** | clues fraction

 Homework

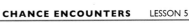 page 40

Designing Mystery Spinner Games

The AllPlay Company would like you to design some new Mystery Spinner Games. You have learned a lot about spinners and probability. Here is a chance for you to use what you know to create games that are fun and challenging.

Design a Mystery Spinner Game

Can you write a set of clues that another student could use to draw a complete spinner?

As a class you will discuss the Unfinished Mystery Spinner. After you have completed the Unfinished Mystery Spinner Game, use the Mystery Spinner Game guidelines to design your own game. When you write your clues, use a separate sheet of paper. Keep the spinner hidden from your classmates.

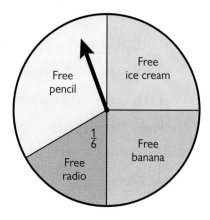

Unfinished Mystery Spinner

Mystery Spinner Game

Spinner Guidelines

- Draw a spinner with 3–5 parts.
- Label the spinner parts with the names of foods, music groups, sports, or whatever you'd like.
- Show the size of each spinner part by labeling it with a fraction, percentage, or decimal.

Clue Guidelines

- Write at least four clues.
- Use a variety of words and numbers to describe the probability of spinning each spinner part.
- Make sure you use fractions, decimals, and percentages to describe probabilities in your clues.
- Make sure your clues tell your classmates everything they need to know to draw your spinner.

Test a Mystery Spinner Game

Try out your partner's Mystery Spinner Game and write your feedback. The goal is to help each other improve the games.

1 Exchange clues with a partner. (Keep the spinner hidden.)

2 Draw a spinner to match your partner's clues.

3 Give your partner feedback on the game by writing answers to these questions:

a. What did you like about the game?

b. What made the game easy or difficult to solve?

c. Were the clues missing any information? If so, what information would you like to get from the clues?

d. What suggestions would you give to improve the game?

> **How can you test a game designed by someone else?**

Tips for Giving Feedback

1. Remember, you are giving feedback to help someone else do a better job or to figure something out.

2. Put yourself in your partner's shoes. What kind of feedback would you find helpful?

Revise the Mystery Spinner Game

Read your partner's feedback on your game. Think about ways to solve any problems.

1 Revise your game. You may need to change your clues and/or your spinner. If your partner drew a spinner that is different from the one you drew, you may want to change your game so that there is only one solution.

2 Write about your game. Include answers to the following questions.

a. How did you improve your game? What changes did you make? Why?

b. What mathematics did you use in your game?

hot **words** | decimal
percent

Homework

page 41

PHASE THREE

The games in this phase are more complex. The results depend on combining the outcomes of two events.

Suppose you have one spinner divided into thirds, with the numbers 1–3, and another spinner divided into fourths, with the numbers 1–4. In a game, Player A gets a point when the sum of two spinner values is odd and Player B gets a point if the sum is even. How might an outcome grid be used to show all the possible combinations in the game?

Fair and Unfair Games

WHAT'S THE MATH?

Investigations in this section focus on:

THEORETICAL and EXPERIMENTAL PROBABILITY

- Conducting probability experiments

- Comparing experimental and theoretical probabilities

- Determining theoretical probability by showing all possible combinations on outcome grids

- Applying probability to determining fairness

MULTIPLE REPRESENTATIONS of PROBABILITY

- Using visual models to analyze theoretical probabilities

- Exploring numerical representations of probabilities and connecting them with visual models

7 Is This Game Fair or Unfair?

EVALUATING THE FAIRNESS OF A GAME

Imagine you are playing a game of chance and you keep losing. You begin to think that the game is unfair, but your opponent insists that it is fair. In this lesson, you will use mathematics to figure out if a game of chance is fair.

Use Outcome Grids to Determine Chances

How can you determine each player's chances of getting points?

Make an outcome grid for the Special Sums Game to show all the possible sums when you roll two number cubes. Follow these directions to make your grid.

1 Draw an outcome grid like the one shown and fill in the boxes. Use the grid to figure out the probability of getting each of the sums (2–12). Which sum do you have the best chance of getting?

2 Color or code the grid to show the ways each player can get points. Use a different color or symbol for each player.

3 When you have finished the grid, write about each player's probability of getting points.

Special Sums Game

1. Players take turns rolling two number cubes and adding the two numbers together.

   If the sum is 1, 2, 3, or 4, Player A gets 1 point. If the sum is 5, 6, 7, or 8, Player B gets 1 point. If the sum is 9, 10, 11, or 12, Player C gets 1 point. Players can get points on another player's turn. For example, if any player rolls a sum of 10, Player C gets 1 point.

2. Record the number of points each player gets.

3. Each player gets 5 turns. The player with the most points at the end of 15 turns is the winner.

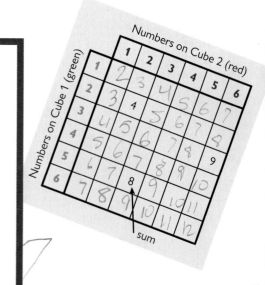

Change the Special Sums Game

If the game is unfair, change the rules to make it fair. If it is fair, then make it unfair. To change the game, follow these steps.

1 Draw a new outcome grid and fill in all the possible sums in the Special Sums Game.

2 How do you want to change the rules? Use the grid to help you figure out which sums get points for which players. Complete the rules below.

> • Players take turns rolling two number cubes. Add the two numbers.
> • Player A gets 1 point when the sums are _____.
> • Player B gets 1 point when the sums are _____.
> • Player C gets 1 point when the sums are _____.
> • The player with the most points after 15 rolls wins. (Each player gets 5 turns.)

3 Color or code the grid to show the ways each player can get a point.

When you have finished changing the game, explain why your new game is fair or unfair.

How can you change a game to make it fair or unfair?

hot **words** | fair
outcome grid

Homework

page 42

8 Charting the Chances

Sometimes games that look fair are really unfair.
Sometimes the opposite is true. How can you determine which games are fair? In this lesson, you will collect data and use outcome grids to analyze spinner, coin, and number-cube games.

How can you determine whether a variety of games are fair?

Investigate the Fairness of Different Games

You will be given several different games to play with a partner or in groups of three. Your challenge is to figure out whether these games are fair or unfair. For each game, follow these steps:

1 Make predictions. Before you play the game, predict whether it is fair or unfair. If you think the game is unfair, which player do you think has the advantage? Write about your thinking.

2 Collect data. Play the game and record your results.

3 Make an outcome grid for the game. Color or code the grid to show each player's probability of getting a point.

4 Describe each player's probability of getting a point in one of these ways: fraction, decimal, or percentage.

5 Write your conclusions. Explain your thinking about whether the game is fair or unfair.

Hint: Some of the games use two game pieces. Others use one, such as a spinner that players spin twice. For games with one piece, you can use the top of the outcome grid for the first spin or toss and the side of the outcome grid for the second spin or toss.

Make an Unfair Game Fair

No one wants to play the Sneaky Sums Game because it is unfair. The AllPlay Company would like you to make the game fair. Read the handout Sneaky Sums Game.

How could you change the rules to make the game fair?

1 On Centimeter Grid Paper, make an outcome grid to find out how unfair the game is. What is each player's probability of getting a point?

2 Change the rules to make the game fair. Which sums do you want to score points for which players? Write your new rules.

3 Color or code the grid to show how each player can get points with your new rules. Describe each player's probability of getting points in two of these ways: fractions, decimals, or percentages.

When you are finished, describe how you changed the rules to make the game fair.

Write About Outcome Grids

How would you teach someone else about outcome grids? Write a letter to a student who will have this unit next year. Share what you have learned about outcome grids. Use one of the games you played in this lesson as an example. Make sure to include answers to these questions in your letter:

- How can you figure out how to set up an outcome grid for a game? How would you label the top and side of the grid? How can you figure out how many boxes the grid should have?

- How can you use an outcome grid to figure out a player's probability of getting points?

- How can you use an outcome grid to figure out if a game is fair?

- What are some mistakes that people might make when they are setting up an outcome grid for a game? How can you avoid those mistakes?

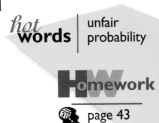

hot **words** | unfair
probability

Homework

page 43

9 Which Game Would You Play?

COMPARING THE CHANCES OF WINNING

Which of four unfair games do you have the best chance of winning? To decide, you will use fractions, decimals, and percentages to describe and compare probabilities. Then you will analyze the Carnival Collection booths from Lesson 1.

Rank Probability Grids for Unfair Games

How can you compare chances of scoring in games with different numbers of outcomes?

You can picture the probability of winning a game by shading a grid. This grid shows that the probability of winning this game is $\frac{6}{36}$ or $\frac{1}{6}$.

$\frac{1}{6}$ [grid]

1 Look at Grids for Unfair Games. Describe Terry's probability of getting a point in each game in at least two different ways: fractions, decimals, or percentages.

2 Rank the grids from "Best for Terry" to "Worst for Terry" (best is a 1). How did you figure out how to rank the grids?

3 For each game, how many points do you think Terry would be likely to get in 100 turns? How many points would Kim be likely to get? Explain your thinking.

4 Make a grid that is better for Terry than the second-best game, but not as good as the best game.

Grids for Unfair Games

Here are grids for four different unfair games. If you were Terry, which game would you want to play?

A   B   C   D

☐ Kim gets a point

▨ Terry gets a point

Compare Carnival Collection Probabilities

How can you use what you have learned to compare probabilities?

Read over the rules for the Coin and Cube Booth and Teens Only Booth in the Carnival Collection on page 6. Then complete the following:

1 What is the probability of scoring a point at the Coin and Cube Booth? at the Teens Only Booth?

    a. Make an outcome grid for each booth. Color or code the grid to show a player's probability of getting a point.

    b. Describe the theoretical probability of scoring a point in three ways: fractions, decimals, and percentages.

2 How many points do you think you would get at the Coin and Cube Booth and the Teens Only Booth for the following number of turns? Explain how you made your predictions.

    a. 36 turns

    b. 72 turns

    c. 100 turns

    d. 1,800 turns

3 Make a probability line to show the theoretical probability of scoring a point at each of the six booths. Rank the booths from best to worst chances of scoring a point (best is 1).

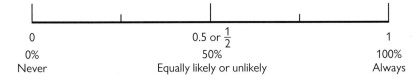

0	0.5 or $\frac{1}{2}$	1
0%	50%	100%
Never	Equally likely or unlikely	Always

4 At each booth, if a player does *not* score a point, it means that the booth owner wins. Change the rules of the Teens Only Booth so that it is almost equally fair for the player and the booth owner. Write your new rules and explain why your version is more fair.

hot **words** | rank
theoretical probability

HW**omework**

page 44

PHASE FOUR

Many games are designed to simulate things that people really do. For example, there are computer games that simulate flying a plane or planning a city. Each of these games captures, in a simple way, some of the events in the actual activity and the probabilities of those events happening.

Think about a familiar activity. How could you design a simulation that is like the real-world activity?

Real-World Simulations

WHAT'S THE MATH?

Investigations in this section focus on:

THEORETICAL and EXPERIMENTAL PROBABILITY

- Conducting probability experiments
- Collecting and analyzing data to determine the probabilities of real-world events
- Using grid models to represent and analyze theoretical probabilities

MULTIPLE REPRESENTATIONS of PROBABILITY

- Representing probability verbally, visually, and numerically

MODELING SITUATIONS with SIMULATIONS

- Modeling the probabilities of real-world events by creating simulations
- Testing simulations by comparing the probabilities of events in a simulation and its real-world counterpart
- Applying probability and statistics to making simulations more realistic

10 Is the Simulation Realistic?

The AllPlay Company has designed a new Miniature Golf Simulation game. A simulation is a game that is like a real activity. The *events* in a simulation should also happen in the real activity. The likelihood of events in the simulation should be the same as their likelihood in the real activity.

Play a Simulation Game

How can you collect data on how often each event occurs in the simulation?

Play the Miniature Golf Simulation with your group. The group will need the Miniature Golf Simulation, Miniature Golf Score Sheet, and two different-colored number cubes.

Miniature Golf Simulation

- Players take turns. On your turn, roll the number cubes and read the game grid to find out how many strokes it took to get the ball in the hole. Each roll of the cubes is considered a stroke.

- Record the number of strokes on your score sheet.

- The player with the least number of points after 18 holes wins.

How to Read the Game Grid

If you roll a 3 on the red cube and a 2 on the green cube, you will get a "Wimpy Putt" and score 3 points. That means it took you 3 strokes to get the ball in the hole. In miniature golf, low scores are better than high scores.

Compare Simulation Data to Actual Data

How can you compare the probabilities in the simulation to the actual sport?

Refer to the handout Actual Miniature Golf Games to complete the following items.

1 Look at the scores on the frequency graphs your class made after playing the simulation. How do the class scores from the simulation compare with the scores on the graph on the handout for the actual game?

2 Complete the table by figuring out the Average Times per Game and the Experimental Probability for each event.

$$\text{average times per game} = \frac{\text{total occurrences}}{\text{number of games}}$$

$$\text{experimental probability for each event} = \frac{\text{total times each event happened}}{\text{total number of holes played}}$$

3 Compare the experimental probabilities of the actual game to the theoretical probabilities of events in the simulation.

a. Use the data from the table you completed in item **2** to rank the events from most likely to least likely.

b. Figure out the theoretical probabilities of events using the Miniature Golf Simulation. Rank the theoretical probabilities of events from most likely to least likely to occur.

4 How realistic is the simulation? Use data to support your conclusions.

Revise the Simulation

Use the data from the actual miniature golf games to design a more realistic simulation.

- Make a new grid for the simulation. How many boxes do you want to give each event?

- What is the theoretical probability of each event in your new simulation?

- Write a description telling how you decided what changes to make.

Are players more likely to get a hole-in-one in the simulation or the actual game?

hot **words** | frequency graph
statistics

page 45

11 The Shape Toss Game

DESIGNING
A SIMULATION
OF A GAME

What are the steps involved in designing a simulation? To find out, you will play a tossing game. You will analyze data your class gathers. Figuring out how many boxes on a grid to give each event helps make the simulation realistic.

Collect Data on a Tossing Game

How can you collect class data for a tossing game?

Play the Shape Toss Game. To record your results, make a table like the one shown.

How can you compile and analyze the class data?

The Shape Toss Game

1. Each group needs the Shape Toss Game Board and a penny for each player to toss.

2. Each player gets at least 5 turns to toss the penny onto the board.

3. Players score the following points if the penny lands inside one of the shapes on the board:

   - Lands in a triangle = 20 points
   - Lands in a rectangle = 10 points
   - Lands in a hexagon = 5 points
   - Misses = 0 points

4. Players record their results.

Sample Table

Player	Triangle (20 pts.)	Rectangle (10 pts.)	Hexagon (5 pts.)	Miss (0 pts.)	Total Score
Corey	0	2	1	2	25 pts
Delia	1	2	2	1	50 pts
Miguel	2	0	2	2	50 pts
Totals	3	4	5	5	125 pts

Design a Simulation of the Tossing Game

How can you use class data to design a realistic simulation of the tossing game?

In the Shape Toss Game, there are four possible events: land in a triangle, land in a rectangle, land in a hexagon, and miss. Follow these steps to analyze the class data and figure out the probability of each event.

1 Copy and complete a table like the one shown so that it has your class's data.

Table of Our Class's Data for the Shape Toss Game			
Number of students who played: _____			
Total number of tosses: _____ (Each student got 5 tosses.)			
Average score: _____			
Event	**Total Times the Event Happened**	**Average Times the Event Happened per Student**	**Experimental Probability of Event**
Triangle			
Rectangle			
Hexagon			
Miss			

2 Make a probability line to rank the events from least likely to most likely.

3 Draw a blank, 36-box grid for your simulation of the Shape Toss Game. Use the class data to help you figure out how many boxes to give each event. Remember that the probabilities of events in the simulation should match as closely as possible the probabilities from actually playing the game.

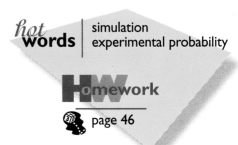

hot **words** | simulation
experimental probability

Homework

 page 46

12 Real-World Simulation Game

FINAL PROJECT

Now it's your turn to design your own simulation. This final project brings together all that you have learned about probability and statistics in this unit. It's exciting to create, test, revise, present, and reflect about your own simulation game.

Brainstorm Ideas

How can you design a simulation of a real-world activity?

Design a simulation game. When you have completed all the steps, use the Project Cover Sheet to summarize your project.

1. Plan your simulation game. Choose a real-world activity to simulate. Describe your ideas and how you will collect data using the Project Planning Sheet.

2. Collect data on the real-world activity. Display the data you collected and describe how you collected it. Write a summary of what you found out.

3. Make a probability line. Use your data to rank the likelihood of the real-world events from least likely to most likely.

4. Design a grid game board for your simulation. Decide which two game pieces (cubes, spinners, etc.) you will use to play your simulation. Draw a blank grid with the appropriate number of boxes. Fill in your grid to make a realistic simulation. Color or code the events.

5. Describe the probabilities of events in your simulation. Use fractions, percentages, or decimals.

6. Write the rules. What is the goal? How do players score points? When does the game end? You may want to design a score sheet.

7. Try out your simulation game. Play it at least twice and record the results. Describe what happened when you played. This isn't an accurate test of the simulation, but it will give you a sense of what it's like to play.

Test the Simulations

Trade games with a partner and play your partner's simulation to test it. Write answers to these questions to give your partner feedback.

- What do you like about the simulation?
- What suggestions would you like to give the game designer?
- How realistic is the simulation?

> ### Giving Constructive Feedback
>
> Here are some ways to give feedback that will help your classmates improve their simulations.
>
> "I really like how you did...."
>
> "Some things you could improve are...."
>
> "I had trouble understanding what you meant by...."
>
> "The part that seemed unclear to me was...."

How did your partner make the simulation realistic?

Reflect on the Projects

Think about the experiences you had when you designed your simulation game and your partner tested it. Consider these questions as you write about your experiences.

- What did you find out when other students tested your simulation?
- What do you like best about your simulation?
- How would you change your simulation to make it more realistic?
- How would you change your simulation to make it more fun to play?
- What tips would you give to other students who wanted to make a realistic simulation game?

hot **words** | natural variability
law of large numnbers

H♦**mework**

 page 47

The Carnival Collection

Applying Skills

In the Get Ahead Booth, you score a point if your coin comes up heads.

1. Predict what your score would be if you played 40 turns at Get Ahead. Explain your prediction.

2. Predict what your score would be if you played 500 turns at Get Ahead. Explain your prediction.

3. Use a coin to play 40 turns at Get Ahead. How many points did you score? Compare your actual results to your predictions for 40 turns.

4. The Tally Sheet shows the points scored in 10 turns at several booths. Which booth would you choose to go to? Why?

Tally Sheet

Lucky Spins	IIII
Big Four	II
Toss 'n' Roll	I
No Doubles	THL III

Extending Concepts

At a new booth called Five or More, you roll a number cube and score a point if you get a 5 or 6.

5. How many points do you think a player would be likely to get in 30 turns at the Five or More Booth? Explain your reasoning.

6. Two students each played 30 turns at the Five or More Booth and recorded their scores in this table. How does each player's score compare with your prediction?

Student	Number of Points Scored
Raphael	8
Sabitra	13

7. How could you change the rules of Five or More so that players would be more likely to want to play it?

8. Design a booth for the Carnival Collection that uses a number cube or coin. Which gives the better chance of scoring points, your booth or Five or More? Why do you think so?

Making Connections

9. Nim is a game for two players that originated in China thousands of years ago. In one variation of Nim, 15 match sticks are laid in a row.

Each player in turn removes 1, 2, or 3 match sticks. The player who is forced to take the last match stick is the loser. Do you think that this game involves chance, skill, or both? Explain your thinking.

Coins and Cubes Experiment

Applying Skills

Find the experimental probability of scoring a point. Express your answers as fractions.

1. A person at the Get Ahead Booth scores 31 points in 50 turns.

2. A person at the Evens and Odds Booth scores 27 points in 72 turns.

3. A person at the Lucky 3s Booth scores 10 points in 49 turns.

4. The strip graph shows what happened when Elena played 10 turns at Lucky 3s. A point is shown by a shaded square.

  a. How many times did she score?

  b. What is her experimental probability of scoring a point?

5. Twelve people each played 10 turns at the Get Ahead Booth. The frequency graph shows how many points each player got.

```
        X       (X: one person's results)
      X X
    X X X X
    X X X X       X
  ─────────────────────
  1 2 3 4 5 6 7 8 9 10
        Number of Wins
```

  a. What was the lowest number of points?

  b. What was the highest number of points?

  c. What was the most common number of points?

Extending Concepts

Five people each played 10 turns at a carnival booth and recorded their data on these strip graphs. A point is shown by a shaded square.

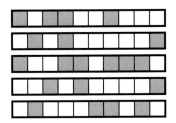

6. Make a frequency graph to show how many points each person got.

7. What is the most common number of points? the average number of points?

8. Combine the data from all five strip graphs to figure out the experimental probability of getting a point.

Writing

9. Answer the letter to Dr. Math.

> Dear Dr. Math,
>
> I don't get it! My friend and I each flipped a coin 10 times. My friend got 8 heads and I got only 2 heads. We thought that we each had a 50% chance of getting heads, but neither of us got 5 heads! Why did this happen? Should we practice flipping coins?
>
> Sooo Confused

From Never to Always

Applying Skills

These four names of students are put in a box: Mica, Syed, Anna, and Jane. One name is picked from the box, and that person wins a prize. Find the theoretical probability that the winner's first name:

1. starts with a vowel

2. contains an *e*

3. contains a vowel

4. has more than four letters

5. does not end with an *e*

6. Order the theoretical probabilities of the five events above from least likely to most likely by placing them on a probability line. Write the probability as a fraction or percentage.

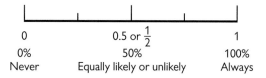

0	0.5 or $\frac{1}{2}$	1
0%	50%	100%
Never	Equally likely or unlikely	Always

In the Get Ahead Booth, you score a point if your coin comes up heads. In the Lucky 3s Booth, you score a point if you roll a 3 on a number cube. Here are the results for 12 turns at each booth.

Get Ahead: T, T, H, T, H, H, T, H, T, H, H, H

Lucky 3s: 1, 4, 2, 5, 3, 6, 1, 4, 3, 5, 1, 2

7. Find the experimental probability of scoring a point at each booth. Give each answer as a fraction, a decimal, and a percentage.

Extending Concepts

8. Read the ad and answer the following questions.

a. Do you think this is a good deal? Why or why not?

b. What do you think your chances of winning would be?

Making Connections

9. A **tetrahedron** is a geometric figure with four identical sides. An **octahedron** has eight identical sides. Suppose you have a tetrahedron die whose sides are numbered 1 to 4 and an octahedron die whose sides are numbered 1 to 8. What is the probability of rolling a 1 on each die? Explain your thinking.

Tetrahedron   Octahedron

Spin with the Cover-Up Game

Applying Skills

Draw a circular spinner for each pair of conditions. Label each part with a fraction.

1. Green and yellow are the only colors. You have an equal chance of spinning green or yellow.

2. You will spin yellow about half of the time. You have an equal chance of spinning red or blue.

3. You are twice as likely to spin green as yellow. You will spin yellow about $\frac{1}{3}$ of the time.

4. Which spinner shown below gives you the best chance of landing on "Striped"? Use a fraction to describe the probability.

5. Which spinner shown below gives you the highest probability of landing on "Dotted"? Use a fraction to describe the probability.

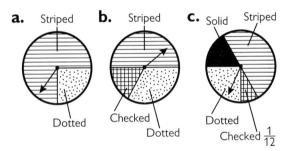

a. Striped / Dotted

b. Striped / Checked / Dotted

c. Solid / Striped / Dotted / Checked $\frac{1}{12}$

Extending Concepts

Suppose you are playing the Cover-Up Game using the spinner shown. Each time the spinner lands on a color, players make an X in the box of that color on their game cards.

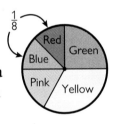

$\frac{1}{8}$ Red / Green / Blue / Pink / Yellow

6. Find the probability of getting each color on the spinner.

7. Make a 24-box game card that would give you a good chance of finishing the game in the fewest possible spins. Explain your thinking.

8. Make a 24-box game card that would give you a poor chance of finishing the game in the fewest possible spins. (The card should still allow you to finish the game.)

Writing

9. Answer the letter to Dr. Math.

Dear Dr. Math,

I can't seem to win at the Cover-Up Game. When I make my game card, I put the colors or words that I think will come up the most in the boxes near the center of the card. I put the ones that won't come up much in the corners. This strategy doesn't seem to work well. Can you suggest a better one?

Wants T. Winn

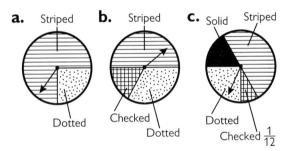

The Mystery Spinner Game

Applying Skills

Find the probability of green, red, and yellow for each spinner.

1.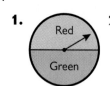

2.

3.

Draw a spinner for each set of parts and label the parts. If the parts cannot be used to make a spinner, explain why not.

4. $\frac{1}{2}, \frac{1}{4}, \frac{1}{8}, \frac{1}{8}$ **5.** $\frac{1}{3}, \frac{1}{4}, \frac{1}{4}, \frac{1}{6}$ **6.** $\frac{1}{3}, \frac{1}{12}, \frac{3}{4}$

7. Design a spinner to match the following clues. Label the parts with fractions.

- There are four pizza toppings.
- You will get pepperoni about 25% of the time.
- You will get pineapple about 30 times in 180 spins.
- You are twice as likely to get onion as pineapple.
- You have the same chances of getting mushroom as pepperoni.

Extending Concepts

8. At Jamila's Unusual Ice Cream Shop, customers can spin a spinner to try to win a free cone. If they do not win a free cone, they must buy the flavor they land on. Draw a spinner that matches these clues. Label the parts with fractions.

- There are three possible flavors.
- Free cone is half as likely as walnut.
- The chance of getting kiwi is 1:4.
- You will get pumpkin about 15 out of 40 times.

9. What's wrong with this set of clues? Describe what is wrong and change the clues. Draw the spinner to match your corrected clue set.

- There are four trips you could win.
- You will win a trip to New Zealand about 7 times out of 20 spins.
- You have a 20% chance of winning a trip to Hawaii.
- You are twice as likely to win a trip to Paris as a trip to Hawaii.
- You are more likely to win a trip to Alaska than a trip to Hawaii.

Writing

10. Answer the letter to Dr. Math.

Peeta ♥

> Dear Dr. Math,
> My friend and I are arguing about the Cover-Up Game. She says she can make a new spinner and a game card with 12 boxes so that she will always cover the card in exactly 12 spins. That doesn't seem possible to me, but she insists she can. How can she do it?
> Ida N. Know

Designing Mystery Spinner Games

Applying Skills

Write at least three clues to describe each spinner. Use different ways to describe the probabilities—fractions, decimals, or percentages.

1.

2.

3.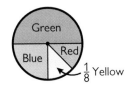

Extending Concepts

David designed the spinner shown and wrote the following clues to describe it.

- There are four colors.

- You have the highest chance of getting green.

- The chances of getting yellow are the same as the chances of getting red.

- You are twice as likely to get blue as red.

David's clues do not give enough information for someone else to draw exactly the same spinner.

4. Draw a spinner that matches David's clues, but is different from his spinner. Label each part with a fraction.

5. Write a new set of clues that gives all the information needed for someone else to draw David's spinner.

Making Connections

The table shows the names and sizes of four deserts in different parts of the world. Sizes are given to the nearest 10,000 square miles.

Desert	Location	Size (mi²)
Arabian	Egypt	70,000
Chihuahuan	Mexico, United States	140,000
Sonoran	Mexico, United States	70,000
Taklimakan	China	140,000

6. Draw a spinner with one part for each desert in the table. Let the size of each spinner part correspond to the size of the desert. For example, the spinner part for the Chihuahuan Desert should be twice as big as the part for the Arabian Desert.

7. Show the size of each part by labeling it with a fraction or percentage.

8. Write at least four clues to describe your spinner. Use words and numbers to describe the probability of spinning each part. Make sure your clues give all the information needed to draw your spinner.

Is This Game Fair or Unfair?

Applying Skills

In the Spinner Sums Game, players spin the two spinners shown and add the two numbers. Player A gets a point if the sum is a one-digit number. Player B gets a point if the sum is a two-digit number. The player with the most points after 15 turns wins.

 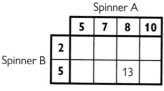

Spinner A   Spinner B

	Spinner A			
	5	**7**	**8**	**10**
2				
5			13	

Spinner B

1. Make an outcome grid like the one shown. Fill in all the sums.

2. List all the different sums you can get. What is the probability of getting each of the sums when you spin the two spinners?

3. Color or code the grid to show the way each player can get points.

4. What is each player's probability of getting a point?

5. Is the game fair or unfair? Explain why.

Extending Concepts

Imagine that you did an experiment where you tossed two number cubes 1,800 times and recorded the number of times you got each sum. Use an outcome grid that shows all the possible sums when you roll two number cubes to help you answer these questions.

6. Which sum or sums would you get the most? the least? Why?

7. Which of these bar graphs do you think your results would look the most like? Why?

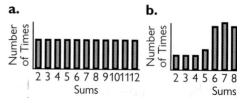
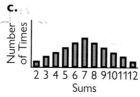

a.   b.

c.

8. How many 9s do you think you would get? Why?

9. How many 3s do you think you would get? Why?

Making Connections

Each number in the *Fibonacci Sequence* is the sum of the previous two:
1, 1, 2, 3, 5, 8, …

A prime number has no factors other than 1 and itself: 2, 3, 5, 7, …

In Roll Again, players roll two number cubes. Player A gets a point if the sum is in the Fibonacci Sequence. Player B gets a point if the sum is a prime number, but not in the Fibonacci Sequence. Player C gets a point otherwise. The player with the most points after 20 turns wins.

10. Make an outcome grid for this game.

11. Color or code the grid to show the way each player scores points.

12. Who do you think will win? Why?

Charting the Chances

Applying Skills

1. An outcome grid for two coin flips is shown below. Use the grid to find the probability that you will get:

a. two heads

b. one head and one tail

c. two tails

d. the same result on both coins

Penny

	H	**T**
H	HH	HT
T	TH	TT

Dime

2. Draw an outcome grid for a game in which you flip a coin and roll a number cube. Use the grid to find the probability that you get:

a. heads and a 3

b. tails and an even number

Extending Concepts

In the Spin and Roll game, players roll a number cube and spin the spinner shown. They use the two numbers that show up to make the *smallest* two-digit number they can. For example, a player who rolls a 4 and spins a 3 will make the number 34.

Player A gets a point if the number is less than 20. Player B gets a point if the number is more than 40. Player C gets a point if the number is between 20 and 40.

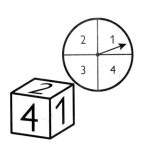

3. Make an outcome grid for Spin and Roll.

4. Color or code the grid to show how each player scores points.

5. Describe each player's probability of getting points as a fraction, decimal, and percentage.

6. Change the rules to make this game fair for three players. Explain your thinking.

7. Write a set of rules that makes this a fair game for four players.

Writing

8. Answer the letter to Dr. Math.

Dear Dr. Math,

I designed a number-cube game called Double or Nothing. Players roll two cubes. They win a prize if they get doubles. I need to figure out how many prizes to buy. I expect that the game will be played about 200 times. About how many prizes do you think I will give out? Tell me how you figured it out, so that I can do it myself next time.

Booth Owner

Which Game Would You Play?

Applying Skills

These numbers represent probabilities of winning different games.

11:25	2 out of 5	84%	0.12

1. For each probability, make a 5-by-5 grid on Centimeter Grid Paper. Fill in the boxes to show each probability.

2. Rank the grids from the best to the worst chances of winning the game.

3. What is the probability of *not* winning for each game?

These outcome grids represent four games. Shaded squares mean Player A gets a point; unshaded squares mean Player B gets a point.

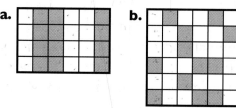

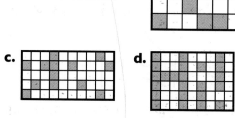

4. Describe Player A's probability of getting a point in each game as a fraction, a decimal, and a percentage.

5. Rank the grids from "Best for A" to "Worst for A."

Extending Concepts

At the Flip and Roll Booth, players flip a coin and roll a number cube. A player scores a point if the coin comes up heads and the cube shows a 1 or 2.

6. Make an outcome grid for Flip and Roll.

7. Shade the grid to show a player's probability of getting a point.

8. How many points do you think you would get at Flip and Roll in 60 turns? in 280 turns? in 2,500 turns? How did you make your predictions?

9. If a player does not get a point, this means that the booth owner wins. Write a new set of rules for Flip and Roll so that it is equally fair for the player and the booth owner. Explain why your version is fair.

Making Connections

The Native American game called *Totolospi* was played by the Moki Indians of New Mexico. Players used flat throwing sticks which were plain on one side and painted on the other. Players would throw three sticks. They scored points if all sticks fell with the same side up.

10. Is it possible to use an outcome grid to find the probability of all sticks falling the same way? Why or why not? If not, can you think of any other way to solve this problem?

Is the Simulation Realistic?

Applying Skills

Two students collected scorecards from a miniature golf course that allows players to take up to six strokes to get the ball in the hole. They used the data to design a new miniature golf simulation. Here is their grid:

- ■ Hole-in-one
- □ Two strokes
- ▦ Three strokes
- ▥ Four strokes
- ▤ Five strokes
- ▧ Six strokes

Green

Red

1. Maylyn rolled a red 5 and a green 2. Which event did she get?

2. What is the theoretical probability of each event in the simulation? Explain how you figured it out.

3. Make a probability line to rank the events in the simulation from least likely to most likely.

4. There are five possible events in the simulation: out, single, double, triple, and home run. Find the theoretical probability of each event.

5. Make a probability line to order the events in the simulation from least likely to most likely.

Compare the simulation to actual data for a professional baseball team.

6. In 6,000 times at bat, the team got 4,200 outs. What is their experimental probability of getting an out? Explain how you figured it out.

7. What is the professional team's experimental probability of getting a home run? In 6,000 times at bat, the team got 180 home runs.

8. How many boxes would you give to outs on the 36-box grid to make the simulation more realistic? How many boxes would you give to home runs? Explain how you found your answers.

Extending Concepts

A simulation baseball game is shown in the outcome grid. The game involves rolling two number cubes.

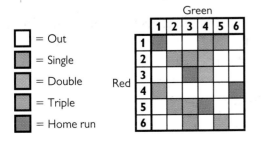

- □ = Out
- ▨ = Single
- ▨ = Double
- ▨ = Triple
- ▨ = Home run

Green

Red

Writing

9. Define *simulation* in your own words.

The Shape Toss Game

Applying Skills

In a simulation, how many boxes would you give to an event on a 40-box outcome grid if its experimental probability is:

1. 25%   **2.** 0.75   **3.** 65%   **4.** 0.48

In the Shape Toss Game, players toss a penny onto a board and score points if the penny lands inside a shape. Here is the data from one class, where the total number of tosses was 90.

Event	Total Times Event Happened in 90 Tosses
Triangle	10
Rectangle	17
Hexagon	20
Miss	43

5. Find the experimental probability of each event.

6. How many boxes would you give each event on a 50-box simulation grid?

Extending Concepts

In the Shape Toss Game shown, players score 20 points for triangles, 10 points for rectangles, 5 points for hexagons, and 0 points for misses.

7. Use your experimental probability data to find the total number of points scored in 90 tosses. How did you figure it out?

8. What was the average number of points scored per toss?

9. Design a simulation of the Shape Toss Game based on the experimental probability of each event.

a. Choose two game pieces to play the game, and make an outcome grid with the appropriate number of boxes.

b. Color or code the grid to give a realistic simulation. Explain how you decided how many boxes to give each event.

c. Play your simulation twice and record the results. Describe what happened.

Writing

10. Answer the letter to Dr. Math.

Dear Dr. Math,

Maria and Carla play on my basketball team. Our coach had to pick a player to take a foul shot. I thought he would pick Maria because she has made 100% of her foul shots this season. But he picked Carla, who has made only 60% of her shots this season. Can you explain this? I thought 100% was better than 60%. Here are their statistics:

Maria	2 shots attempted	2 shots made
Carla	100 shots attempted	60 shots made

Team Manager and Record Keeper

Real-World Simulation Game

Applying Skills

1. For each pair of game pieces below, give the number of boxes in their outcome grid. Then make the grid.

a. two number cubes

b. a number cube and a coin

2. Find the experimental probability of each event in the table. Tell how many boxes you would give to each event in a 6 × 6 outcome grid.

Serves in Ten Games of Tennis

Event	Number of Times
Fault	12
Double fault	6
No fault	24
Ace	6

Extending Concepts

The data in the table refer to the NCAA soccer championships played from 1959 to 1990. The events are the number of goals scored in the final by the winning team.

Number of Goals Scored by Winning Team in Final	Total Goals Scored in 31 Games
1	10
2	10
3	4
4	5
5	2

3. Find the experimental probability of each event. Make a probability line and rank the events from least likely to most likely.

4. Choose two game pieces you will use to play the game. Make an outcome grid with the appropriate number of boxes. Fill in your grid to make a realistic simulation. Explain how you decided how many boxes to give to each event.

5. Write a short set of rules explaining how to use your simulation.

6. What are the probabilities of each event happening in your simulation? Use fractions, decimals, and percentages to describe these probabilities.

Writing

7. Answer the letter to Dr. Math.

Dear Dr. Math,

My friend and I want to design a simulation softball game. We want the scores in the simulation to be like the scores real middle school students get. How can we collect the data we need? How much data should we collect?

Hi Score

STUDENT GALLERY

The Seeing and Thinking Mathematically project is based at Education Development Center, Inc. (EDC), Newton, MA, and was supported, in part, by the National Science Foundation Grant No. 9054677. Opinions expressed are those of the authors and not necessarily those of the National Science Foundation.

CREDITS: Photography: Chris Conroy • Beverley Harper (cover) • Jim Corwin/Photo Researchers: pp. 2TR, 4–5 • © John Callanan/Image Bank: pp. 3TC, 20–21 • Special thanks to Chris Conroy and Golfland USA, Sunnyvale, CA: pp. 3TR, 28–29. Illustrations: Manfred Geier: p. 36BR • Dan Brawner: pp. 7B, 11B, 15TR, 15CL, 23B, 30C, 33B